dabblelab

PROJECT PASSION

BIT by BIT

Projects for Your Odds and Ends

by Mari Bolte

CAPSTONE PRESS

a capstone imprint

Dabble Lab is published by Capstone Press,
1710 Roe Crest Drive, North Mankato, Minnesota 56003
www.mycapstone.com

Library of Congress Cataloging-in-Publication Data is available
on the Library of Congress website.

ISBN: 978-1-5157-7375-7 (library hardover)
ISBN: 978-1-5157-7379-5 (eBook PDF)

Editorial Credits:
Kayla Rossow, designer; Tori Abraham, production specialist

Photo Credits:
All photos by Capstone Studio/Karon Dubke
Background design elements by Shutterstock
Project production by Marcy Morin, Kayla Rossow, Mari Bolte,
and Sarah Schuette

Printed in Canada.
010395F17

Table of Contents

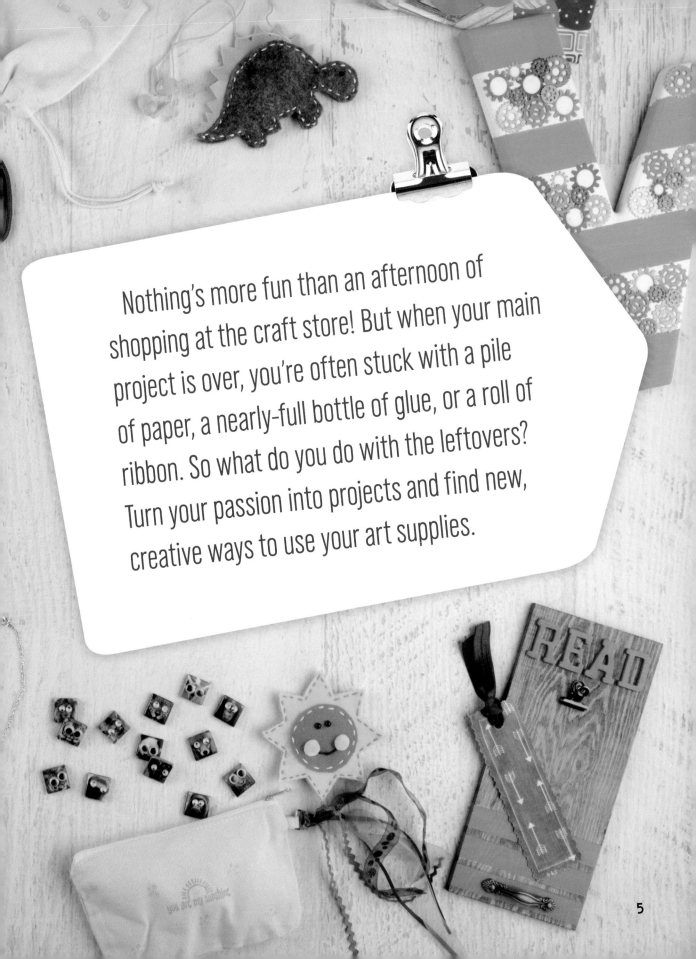

Nothing's more fun than an afternoon of shopping at the craft store! But when your main project is over, you're often stuck with a pile of paper, a nearly-full bottle of glue, or a roll of ribbon. So what do you do with the leftovers? Turn your passion into projects and find new, creative ways to use your art supplies.

Lovely Labels

Display your school ID along with your favorite fabric! A ribbon or thread will keep your ID secure, and everyone will know that you've got style.

Steps:

1. Brush decoupage stiffening glue or white craft glue over fabric and let dry. Turn the fabric over and repeat on the other side. This should make the fabric stiff enough to use with a large paper punch.

2. Punch two shapes out of the fabric.

3. Set one piece of fabric aside. Have an adult help you cut a rectangle out of the second piece. The rectangle piece should be slightly smaller than your ID badge.

4. Stack the fabric pieces together, with the frame piece on top, right-side-up. Use fabric glue or a heavy-duty needle and thread along three edges of the fabric pieces to attach them to each other.

5. Once the glue is dry, slide in your ID. Use a small hole punch near the open end of the tag. Loop a ribbon through the hole.

♥ TRY IT!

Variation:

• Follow all the instructions for the ID tags, but make a bookmark instead. Slip a piece of cardstock into the bookmark's pocket in place of the ID. Use the cardstock to write down books you've read and liked. You can also keep track of books on your wish list, or use it as a checklist of things to do.

Tip: If you don't have a craft punch, just make freehand cuts with scissors.

Variation:

• After cutting out one piece of fabric, glue a thin strip of cardstock in the center. When you stiffen the fabric, bend the sides of the fabric around the cardstock to make a book shape. Cut the second piece of fabric in two, and trim to fit either side of the book's inside cover. Cut and fold paper to fit inside, and glue the paper to the book's spine.

♥ TRY IT!

Tip: For a heavier-duty ribbon hole, ask an adult to use a hole punch and eyelet setter to add metal eyelets.

Leftover Letters

Letters are fun for spelling out words or names, but there are always leftovers! What can you do with the extra Xes, Ys, and Zs?

Steps:

1. Glue or tape a piece of fabric onto the backing of a picture frame. Place iron-on letters over the fabric and iron in place.

2. Center a wooden letter of your choice over the backing, and glue into place. Reassemble the frame.

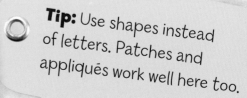

Tip: Use shapes instead of letters. Patches and appliqués work well here too.

• Arrange and stick stickers on the frame's glass. Sponge acrylic or glass paint over and around the stickers. Let the paint dry, and then remove the stickers. Replace the frame's backing to display photos or art.

• Discard the frame's backing, and decorate the entire piece of glass. Then attach it to the frame with industrial-strength glue. Use a suction cup or a ribbon to hang your artwork.

Tip: Ask an adult to help you use a craft knife to remove any stubborn stickers. The knife can also be used to gently scrape stray paint from the glass.

♥ TRY IT!

Variations:

• Use the letters to decorate the wooden letter or the picture frame itself.

• Paint the photo frame for even more color coordination.

Crafty Captures

Capture a favorite fossil, stone, or gem forever with a few simple twists. Experiment with wire thickness, stone shape, and twisty techniques.

Basic Bead

1. Use pliers to bend a simple loop of craft wire about 1 inch (2.5 centimeters) from the end of the wire. Wrap the wire tail around the base of the loop.

2. Center the loop on top of the stone and hold the loop in place with your fingers. Wrap the wire around the stone as many times as you want. (Be sure to wrap to the left and the right of the loop, to keep your stone balanced.)

3. When you're done wrapping, cut the wire and tuck the tail under the wraps.

Tip: Craft wire varies in thickness. The smaller the gauge, the thinner the wire — 22- to 24-gauge works best for this sort of project. Use wire cutters to get a clean cut every time. (Fingernail clippers work fine for thin gauges.) Pliers will ensure you get clean twists and tight wrapping.

Level 2 Loops

Start with step 1, but Instead of many tight wraps together, space them out along the stone. Be sure the stone is secure at its base. When you're done wrapping, use the pliers to twist the end of the wire into a spiraled shape.

Tip: Experiment with your wire loops! Try crossing the wire over itself, or adding twists where overlaps occur.

Captured Pendants

Variation:

• Use the same wiring technique, but string small beads onto the wire, instead of wrapping around a single large stone.

Steps:

1. Select a metal ring with a diameter larger than your stone.

2. Wrap one end of some thinner wire around the metal ring. Tuck the wire's tail under the wraps.

3. Thread the other end of the wire around the opposite side of the ring. Loop once or twice to keep the wire in place.

4. Set your stone in the center of the ring, on top of the thin wire.

5. Criss-cross the thin wire across the ring again so it's near the starting point, but not quite next to it. Make a couple loops to hold the wire in place. Continue criss-crossing and looping, moving the wire over a little bit each time, until the stone is securely held in place by the thin wire.

6. Give the thin wire a couple final loops before cutting it and tucking the end under the wraps.

Well-Rounded Crafter

Sometimes a project will call for a large hole punch, or a pack of a specifically-shaped materials. Go full circle with these well-rounded crafts.

Steps:

1. Arrange felt circles in a pattern of your choosing on top of a pillow. Will you make a row of circles, or overlap them? Alternating colors can be fun. Or just make everything a rainbow!

2. Use fabric glue to attach the circles to the pillow.

Variation:

• Glue pom-poms on top of the circles, or use flatback gems instead. A large sequin on top of each circle would give overlapping circles a more scalelike look.

❤ TRY IT!

Variations:

• Felt in different shades of one color will create a monochromatic look.

• Try fabric or felt strips instead of circles. Weave or layer the fabric strips over the pillow, like a latticed pie crust.

Tip: A wide variety of inexpensive, pre-cut felt circles, in many sizes, can be found online.

Variation:

• Instead of felt, use fabric, scrapbook paper, tissue paper, origami paper, or even photos. Cut out uniform circles or punched shapes, or get creative and make a mosaic with randomly cut pieces. Then glue or decoupage the pieces onto a canvas for instant art.

❤ TRY IT!

Tip: Make this any size you want! Create small cards or big posters. Use large circles or tiny dots, or use a variety for a completely different look.

Air-Dried Display

Air dry clay is easy to use and easy to find. It can be painted, molded, carved, and sculpted. But if you don't use it all right away, it can dry out, leaving you with a useless lump. Get the most out of your clay with these quick and easy crafts.

Recipe: DIY Clay Glaze
clear nail polish
2 tablespoons (30 milliliters) white glue
3 tablespoons (45 mL) water
acrylic paint

Combine all ingredients in a bowl, and mix well. Paint directly on to dried clay.

Steps:

Make a bowl for holding jewelry, pins, or other small bits.

1. Roll out the clay so it's about 0.2 inches (5 millimeters) thick. Set a small glass bowl upside down on the clay, and use a knife to cut around the bowl's edge.

2. Flip the bowl over and press the clay circle into the bowl. Smooth out any lumps, and then leave the clay in the bowl for 24 to 48 hours.

3. After your clay bowl is dry, it should easily pop out of the glass bowl. Decorate with acrylic paint, or use DIY clay glaze.

Tip: You can buy air-dry clay, or make your own. For the most basic recipe, mix two parts corn starch with one part white glue and stir until there are no more lumps.

Variation:

• After you roll out the clay, use a rubber stamp to decorate it. Dip the stamp in paint or ink for extra color, or just paint details on the clay after it is dry.

Use a shaped cookie cutter to make an ornament. Be sure to use a toothpick to make a hole so you can hang it!

♥ TRY IT!

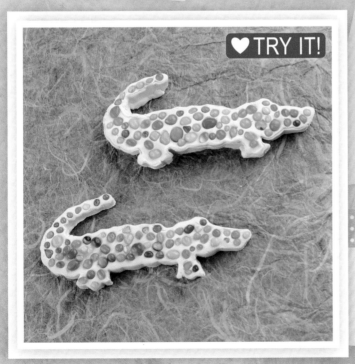

♥ TRY IT!

Tip: You can color the wet clay before or after you sculpt too. Knead acrylic paint into the clay one drop at a time until the desired color is reached.

Variation:

Press found objects, such as shells, buttons, gems, and beads, into wet clay.

15

One-of-a-Kind Creation

Make a memory board using wood stain pens. Learn how to make your own stencil with painter's tape for an extra bit of personalization.

Steps:

1. Completely cover a wooden board with painter's tape. Draw or trace your desired design directly onto the tape. Have an adult cut around your design with a craft knife. Then pull up the tape around the design.

2. Color in the wood with a wood stain pen, or have an adult help you use actual wood stain. Let the wood dry as directed.

3. Attach a metal clip or other hardware to the top and corners of the board.

Variations:

- Use paint instead of — or in addition to — the wood stain or wood stain pens.

- Pull up the taped design itself, instead of the tape around the design.

- Add nails, screws, and other found hardware for a more industrial look.

- You can also use washi or masking tape for this project. Try laying the tape in patterns (such as stripes or geometric designs) instead of cutting out a shape.

- Use one color of wood stain on the whole board. Use another color stain on a wooden letter. Then attach the letter to the board for a 3D look.

❤ TRY IT!

READ

Book Report due tomorrow

Tip: Not sure what to use for a design? Stencils are always easy. But you can also trace regular objects, such as a jar lid, cookie cutter, or precut foam shape.

Statement Stamps

Use stamps and fabric paint to custom-make your very own statement piece. Decorate a bag, T-shirt, towels, socks, or pillow to match your mood. Make one for every day of the week, in every color, and for every person on your gift-giving list.

Steps:

1. Place a piece of craft foam between the fabric and your work surface. If you're stamping a pillow, shirt, or something else with a front and back, place the foam between the fabric's layers.

2. Pour a small amount of fabric paint onto a disposable plate. Dip a sponge paintbrush into the paint, and dab it onto the plate a couple times to get rid of any excess paint. Pat a thin layer of fabric paint evenly onto the stamp with the paintbrush.

3. Press the stamp firmly onto the fabric. Then lift the stamp straight up.

4. Repeat steps 2 and 3 until your fabric is decorated to your liking.

5. Let the paint dry completely. Then turn the fabric over and iron the back of the fabric on high heat for 30 seconds. This will set the paint and make your design washable.

Tip: If your stamped design is meant to be an even pattern, use a ruler and pencil to lightly measure and mark out exactly where each stamp should sit. Use painter's tape to ensure the straightest lines possible.

Variation:

• If stamping isn't your thing, use cotton swabs, chopsticks, or pencil erasers to dot your pattern instead. Wrap rubber bands around a rolling pin, or press on bits of sticky-back foam. Then dab with paint and roll the rolling pin across your fabric.

Tip: You can make your own stamps by carving designs into corks, craft foam, erasers, and firm fruits and vegetables, such as apples or potatoes.

♥ TRY IT!

Variation:

• Use the painter's tape technique on page 16 to create a blank stencil on a piece of canvas board or heavy-duty paper. Use a variety of small stamps to print inside the stencil. Be sure to press down firmly, and try not to overlap the stamp patterns. When you're done stamping and the ink is dry, carefully pull up the painter's tape.

Felt Friends

Make a felt dino friend to take wherever you go.

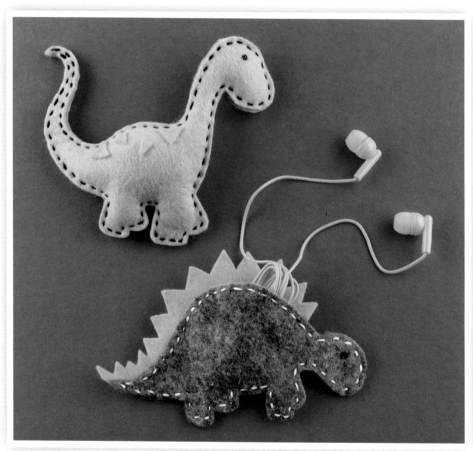

Steps:

1. Sketch out your design on a piece of paper. Start with the larger piece, such as the dino's body. Then add one or more smaller shapes as accent pieces, such as back spikes, teeth, eyes, or colored spots. Once you're happy with your design, trace your design onto felt, and cut it out.

2. Stitch around each piece with contrasting colors of embroidery thread for a color pop.

3. Use a regular needle and thread to sew the dino pieces together. Don't sew all the way around the dino, though — leave a little pocket to store loose change, headphones, and other small items.

4. Use glue to attach accent pieces. Sew on beads for eyes, or add details with paint or permanant marker.

Variations:

- Stuff the dino with batting or fabric scraps. Then sew it shut!

- Alternatively, skip the stuffing but sew all the way around. Then glue your felt friend onto a headband or hair clip.

❤ TRY IT!

Variation:

❤ TRY IT!

- Sketch a large animal shape onto your favorite felt or fabric. Use a regular needle and thread to sew the edges together. Leave the last inch or two unsewn, and turn the animal inside out. Stuff with batting or fabric scraps before sewing completely shut.

Glue or sew on pom-poms for texture and interest. Add extra details, such as ears or collars, with felt or fabric scraps.

21

Ribbon and Lace

No matter what the project, it seems like ribbon never runs out
(unless, of course, there's not quite enough to finish)!
Use up leftover ribbon in surprising and unexpected ways.

Tip: Cover the threaded ends with washi tape or thin strips of duct tape. Use superglue to seal the ends of the tape.

Steps:

1. Cut two 45-inch (114-cm) pieces of ribbon.

2. Tie a piece of thread ½ inch (1.3 cm) from one end of a ribbon. Wrap the thread around the ribbon tightly until you get as close to the end as possible. Tie off the thread and trim off any excess. Repeat at the other end of the ribbon.

3. Coat the threads with clear nail polish. Pay extra-close attention to the ends of the thread.

4. Once the nail polish is dry, trim off any excess thread. Then add another coat of nail polish.

5. Repeat with the second ribbon.

Variation:

• You can also make shoelaces out of bias tape, paracord, or lace.

• Loop a small charm onto the thread as you wrap the ribbon.

22

Ribbon Frame

Don't waste those scrap bits of ribbon! Use what you've trimmed to frame an already-eye-catching piece of art.

How to:

Wrap ribbons around a frame. Use hot glue to attach the ends to the back of the frame. Wrap with one long piece of ribbon, or just many short pieces.

Variations:

• Weave ribbons in a criss-crossing pattern instead of straight across.

• Tie ribbons instead of using glue. Leave the knots facing outward for a larger-than-life look.

• Use fabric scraps instead of ribbon. Or use both! A combination of textures might make things extra-interesting.

A Puzzling Reflection

Check out your craftiness by re-framing a mirror with puzzle pieces.
This quick and easy project will be different every time you make it.

Steps:

1. Center a 5 inch (12.7 cm) round mirror on top of a 10 inch (25.4 cm) round mirror. Use industrial-strength glue to attach the small mirror to the large mirror.

2. Arrange puzzle pieces around the edge of the large mirror. Try stacking pieces on top of each other or using several connected pieces together.

3. When you're happy with your arrangement, glue the puzzle pieces in place with hot glue.

❤ TRY IT!

Variation:

• Try using plastic building blocks instead of puzzle pieces! Use only one type of shape — round, pointed, irregular, or brick — instead of a mixture. Challenge yourself to fit round pieces with square shapes. Where will the weird peices go?

Variation:

• Arrange puzzle pieces in a triangle shape, and glue together. You can paint puzzle pieces before assembly, or have an adult help you spray paint them after. Make large ones as a wall display, or add jewelry settings or earring wires to smaller pieces for pendants or earrings.

Old Crayons

Crayons never seem to disappear! Use up those broken bits to create a splash of art instead.

Steps:

1. Paint a canvas your favorite color.

2. With an adult's help, use a vegetable peeler to create crayon shavings.

3. Scatter shavings across the canvas.

4. Preheat an iron on high heat. Have an adult hold the iron over the canvas — without touching the surface — until the shavings melt completely.

5. Sprinkle glitter over the wet crayon before it sets.

Variation:

- Glue a coloring book page onto the canvas. Trace outlines with black puffy paint. Let the paint dry completely. Place crayon bits between the puffy paint to add color to your picture. Then melt the crayon.

Tip: Use a clean paintbrush to remove any out-of-place crayon shavings.

Variation:

- Have an adult chop crayons with a knife instead of peeling them, to make many different sizes of crayon bits. (This will make some of the pieces harder to melt, though!)

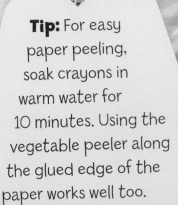

Tip: For easy paper peeling, soak crayons in warm water for 10 minutes. Using the vegetable peeler along the glued edge of the paper works well too.

Re-Tiled

Individually, old tiles aren't very impressive. Maybe they're part of a package left over from another craft. Maybe they're part of a game that can no longer be played because other tiles are missing. Make something of the leftovers with a little paint, decoupage, and love.

Steps:

1. Paint tiles with white acrylic paint. If there are letters or numbers printed on the tiles, that's OK. Just flip the tiles over when it's time to decorate. Let the paint dry completely.

2. Squeeze a large dab of paint onto a disposable plate or bowl. Squeeze out additional dabs of black and white.

3. Paint the tiles with your chosen color, mixed with black and white. Vary the order of paints used, and go over each tile multiple times to make sure the paint is blended for that piece. You should end up with tiles in many different shades of one color. Let the tiles dry completely before using them in crafts.

Variations:

• Glue the tiles down before painting them. Use the same painting technique, but color all the tiles at once.

• Paint the part of the box where the tiles will sit. Use a bright, vivid color, such as gold or silver. When you place the tiles, leave a small space between each one, so the paint shows through.

• Use small coins or stones instead of tiles.

An Eyeful

Get a little crazy with some animal pictures and a pack of googly eyes.

Steps:

1. Cut small animal faces to fit on small tiles.
2. Coat the front of each tile with a thin layer of decoupage glue, and press your images into place. Paint decoupage over the top of the tiles, and set aside for 10 minutes.
3. Have an adult trim any excess paper off with a craft knife. Then apply another layer of decoupage glue. Let dry completely.
4. Cover the tiles with dimensional decoupage. Let dry completely.
5. Glue googly eyes over the animal faces.

Variations:

• Glue a metal bail to the back of each tile to turn them into pendants.

• Glue a magnet to the back of each tile to decorate your refrigerator.

29

Rustic Remnants

Use up leftover hardware, metal bits, scrap electronics, and even unmatched or broken jewelry with a little paint, glue, and inspiration.

Variations:

- Use metal tacks, very short nails, or screws.

- Have an adult help you take apart an old small appliance, such as a toaster. Small appliances are full of useful pieces.

- Small toy cars, trains, model accessories (such as tires, road sections, or train tracks), game pieces, trinkets (such as play jewelry, food, or miniature animals), and building supplies are all great alternatives to hardware pieces.

Steps:

1. Paint a wooden letter with acrylic paint. Once it is dry, use painter's tape to mark off lines.

2. Paint inside the taped lines with a second, darker color. Let the paint dry completely before removing the painter's tape.

3. Glue on your hardware. Add a few small pieces for interest, or cover the entire letter with a variety of pieces.

♥ TRY IT!

Variations:

- Jump rings can connect interesting-looking washers, gears, and nuts. Make a long string for a necklace, or attach them to earring wires for easy DIY jewelry.

- Add beads or charms to the jump rings to add some color.

♥ TRY IT!

Variations:

- Large washers are easy to find in hardware stores. Use spray paint or alcohol ink to color them.

- Use a metal stamping kit on washers to spell out words or messages, phrases, or names.

- Loop a cord or a jump ring around a washer or gear to make a pendant. Try stacking several different sizes on top of each other.

- Thread washers onto split key rings to make keychains instead of necklaces.

♥ TRY IT!

Read More

Harbo, Christopher L. *Sock Puppet Theater Presents Little Red Riding Hood: A Make & Play Production.* North Mankato, Minn.: Capstone Press, 2018.

Hove, Carol. *Make It Yourself! From Junk to Jewelry.* Minneapolis: Abdo Pub., 2017.

Mercer, Bobby. *Junk Drawer Engineering: 25 Construction Challenges that Don't Cost a Thing.* Chicago: Chicago Review Press Incorporated, 2017.

Suen, Anastasia. *Birthday Gifts.* Vero Beach, Flo.: Rourke Educational Media, 2017.

Internet Sites

Use FactHound to find Internet sites related to this book.

Visit *www.facthound.com*

Just type in 9781515773757 and go!

 Check out projects, games and lots more at **www.capstonekids.com**

Maker Space Tips

Download tips and tricks for using this book and others in a library maker space.

Visit *www.capstonepub.com/dabblelabresources*

32